Walt Disney

A Photo-Illustrated Biography

by June Preszler

Consultant:
Jerry Beck
Consulting Editor
Cartoon Research
West Hollywood, California

Bridgestone Books
an imprint of Capstone Press
Mankato, Minnesota

Bridgestone Books are published by Capstone Press
151 Good Counsel Drive, P.O. Box 669, Mankato, Minnesota 56002ʻ
http://www.capstone-press.com

Library of Congress Cataloging-in-Publication Data
Preszler, June, 1954–
  Walt Disney / by June Preszler.
    p. cm.—(Photo-illustrated biographies)
  Summary: A biography of the well-known animator, moviemaker, and theme park creator
whose technological advancements gave us Mickey Mouse and Disneyland.
  ISBN 0-7368-2226-7 (hardcover)
  1. Disney, Walt, 1901–1966—Juvenile literature. 2. Animators—United States—
Biography—Juvenile literature. [1. Disney, Walt, 1901–1966. 2. Motion pictures—Biography.]
I. Title. II. Series.
NC1766.U52D5545 2004
791.43ʹ092—dc21   2003000317

Editorial Credits
Heather Adamson, editor; Steve Christensen, series designer; Enoch Peterson, book
    designer and illustrator; Kelly Garvin, photo researcher; Eric Kudalis, product
    planning editor

Photo Credits
Corbis/Bettman, cover, 4, 8, 10, 12, 16, 18
Getty Images/Hulton Archive, 6, 14
Index Stock Imagery/Peter Adams, 20

1 2 3 4 5 6 08 07 06 05 04 03

Table of Contents

"I happen to be kind of an inquisitive guy and when I see things I don't like, I start thinking why do they have to be like this and how can I improve them."
—Walt Disney, referring to why he created Disneyland

Walt Disney

In the 1940s, Walt Disney took his daughters to amusement parks. He believed he could build a better park that both children and adults could enjoy.

Walt had already created characters like Mickey Mouse, Donald Duck, and Goofy. He had made movies such as *Snow White and the Seven Dwarfs*, *Pinocchio*, and *Bambi*.

Walt imagined a theme park with a Main Street and a castle for Cinderella. His theme park would also need a jungle, a riverboat, a railroad line, and lots of rides.

His amusement park dream turned into Disneyland. It opened July 17, 1955, in California. Later, his ideas for family fun led to an even bigger park. Disney World opened in Orlando, Florida, in 1971.

Walt Disney hosted a live broadcast of Disneyland's opening in 1955.

 # Farm Life

On December 5, 1901, Walt Disney was born to Elias and Flora Disney, in Chicago, Illinois. He had three older brothers. His sister Ruth was born in 1903.

When Walt was 4 years old, the family moved to a farm in Missouri. The Disney children had farm chores each day. Walt took care of the animals. He often drew pictures of the animals.

Walt's drawings sometimes got him in trouble. In school, he would rather doodle than complete his schoolwork. He even carved his initials into his grade school desk.

When Walt was 7, he and his sister found a bucket of sticky, black tar. Walt told Ruth that they could draw on their house with the tar and wash it off later. When they tried to remove the pictures, the tar had dried. The drawings were still there in 1911 when the family moved to Kansas City.

Walt Disney was born in Chicago on December 5, 1901. He spent most of his childhood in Missouri.

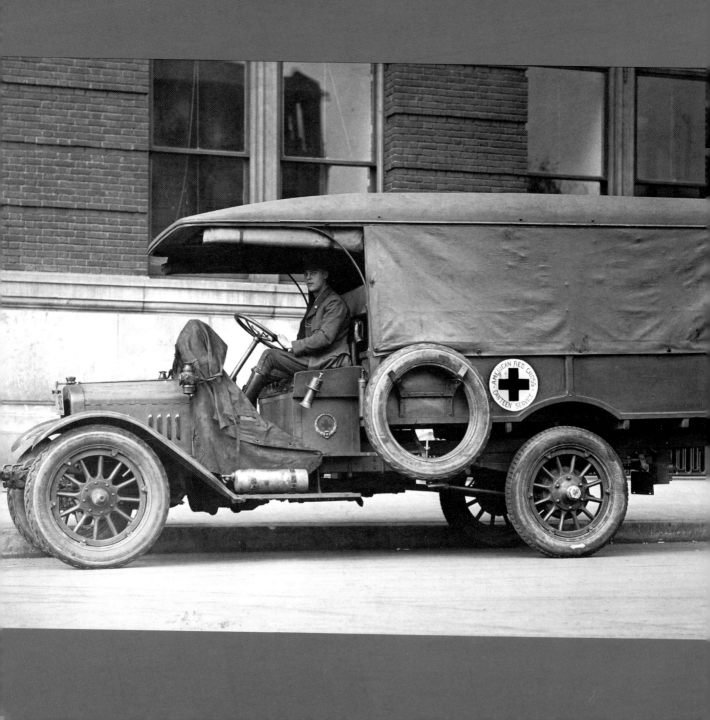

Growing Up

In Kansas City, Walt's father owned a large paper route. Walt and his brother woke at 3:30 each morning to deliver newspapers before school.

Six years later, Walt's family moved back to Chicago. By this time, World War I (1914–1918) had begun. Walt became more interested in the war than in anything else. He wanted to find a way to help.

At 16, Walt was too young to be a soldier. But the Red Cross Ambulance Corps accepted 17-year-olds. Walt lied about his age and volunteered.

He was sent to France as the war ended. Walt was one of 50 young men chosen to help with cleanup efforts. Walt also helped wounded soldiers.

Walt continued to use his art skills. He drew pictures on the Red Cross ambulances. Walt and a friend also made money by decorating helmets.

Trucks like these were used by the Red Cross Ambulance Corps in World War I.

"I'll make the name Disney famous around the world."
—Walt Disney to his father in the early 1920s

Living His Dream

Late in 1919, Walt returned to Kansas City to begin an art career. First, he worked for an advertising company as an apprentice to learn the business. But the company's sales went down, and they could not pay him. Walt and a friend, Ub Iwerks, decided to start their own art business. Their business did not make much money.

In the early 1920s, Walt and Ub went to work for the Kansas City Slide Company. They became involved in making cartoon characters move across a movie screen. This was called animation. It was just beginning to take over the cartoon world.

Once again, Walt had some ideas of his own. He decided to make funny cartoons about things that were important to people in Kansas City. He sold his cartoon Laugh-O-Grams to a local theater. The cartoons became a hit.

Walt sketched cartoon ideas at his drawing table.

To California

Laugh-O-Grams gave Walt confidence. He hired more artists. When the team's first big project turned out well, Walt quit his job to make cartoons.

Many people wanted Walt's cartoons, but Walt was not a good businessperson. Too often, he made deals on trust. Some companies did not pay Walt for his work. Soon, his company was in trouble.

Walt decided to move to California. He wanted to be near his brother Roy and work in the exciting world of movies. Walt and Roy became partners. They started the Disney Brothers Studio in 1923.

The studio produced silent films called the Alice Comedies. Walt also created Oswald the Lucky Rabbit. This character later inspired Mickey Mouse.

Walt fell in love with Lilly Bounds, one of his employees. They married on June 13, 1925. In 1933, their daughter, Diane was born. The couple adopted another daughter, Sharon, in 1937.

Walt and Lilly went sledding together at a children's event in 1933.

Mickey, Snow White, and More

In 1928, Walt began work on his most popular character, a mouse named Mickey. On November 18, 1928, Mickey Mouse was featured in "Steamboat Willie." It was the first cartoon that had sound to match the picture. Mickey was a success.

During the 1930s, Walt and the studio created friends to join Mickey. Soon, Donald, Minnie, Goofy, and Pluto became cartoon stars. Walt also used Mickey Mouse to promote another series called *Silly Symphonies*. These cartoons were set to classical music. The *Silly Symphony*, "Flowers and Trees," was the first cartoon ever produced in color.

Walt then decided to create a full-length cartoon movie. People thought no one would watch a cartoon that long. But crowds of people went to theaters to see *Snow White and the Seven Dwarfs*. *Pinocchio, Fantasia, Dumbo,* and *Bambi* followed.

**Walt holds drawings from *Snow White* and *Bambi*.
He was the first to make full-length animated movies.**

"I was the only studio in town that was practically a war plant."
—Walt Disney on the takeover of his studio during World War II by the U.S. Army

The War Effort

In 1941, Walt's studio was busy making cartoons and animated films. Everything changed when the United States joined World War II (1939–1945) that same year.

Seven hundred U.S. Army soldiers soon took over Walt's studio. They protected a nearby aircraft plant important to the war effort. The soldiers stayed for eight months.

Walt's studio stopped making its cartoons. Instead, the studio made films for the military. Walt made training films and special war cartoons.

After the war, Walt decided to try new things. He started a nature series, *True-Life Adventures*. He also began producing live-action films that featured real actors. But he did not give up on animation. The company released *Cinderella* in 1950. It has become one of Disney's most popular films.

Walt uses a storyboard to explain a new war cartoon idea to U.S. government officials.

The Disneyland Dream

Walt was not satisfied only making movies. He wanted to build a theme park. Walt paid for his dream by creating a TV show with ABC Television.

The show, *Disneyland*, began in 1954. People watched it in black-and-white. But Walt filmed it in color. He knew that one day people would watch color TV. Other popular shows of the 1950s like *Davy Crockett* and *Zorro* had their beginnings on *Disneyland*.

The Disneyland theme park opened in 1955. Walt wanted to wait to open the park. He knew the park was not ready. But the tickets were already sold.

The park opening was a disaster. People sneaked into the park. Traffic jammed roads. Rides did not work. Guests could not find the rest rooms. Still, visitors kept coming. The problems were fixed, and the first theme park became a magical success.

Walt hosted a weekly television show called *Disneyland*. The show helped pay for building the park.

"It's kind of fun to do the impossible."
—Walt Disney on the creation of Disneyland and other projects people
said he could not do

The Magic Continues

Walt kept making TV shows and movies, but he never stopped trying new things. He created a TV show just for kids called *The Mickey Mouse Club*. The movie, *Mary Poppins*, had live actors, cartoon characters, and special effects all in one film.

Walt wanted to build another theme park. He made plans for creating Disney World in Orlando, Florida. This park would include a city of the future called EPCOT.

Walt did not live to see Disney World and EPCOT. He died from cancer on December 15, 1966. Plans for Disney World continued. The park opened in 1971. EPCOT opened in 1982.

Walt Disney's projects remain popular today. The studio still tries new things and makes new movies and shows. People from around the world visit Walt's theme parks. Mickey, Donald, and Goofy still bring smiles to children and adults.

The EPCOT Center uses new technology and design. Walt wanted EPCOT to be a model for new cities.

Fast Facts about Walt Disney

 In 1928, Walt Disney wanted to name his cartoon mouse "Mortimer." Walt's wife, Lilly, talked him into "Mickey Mouse."

 Walt is the Academy of Motion Picture Arts and Sciences' most honored individual. He has been awarded 26 Oscars.

 In making *Bambi*, Walt required his artists to study live deer. He wanted the cartoon animals to behave like real deer.

Dates in Walt Disney's Life

1901—Walt Disney is born on December 5, in Chicago.

1906—The Disney family moves to a Missouri farm.

1918—Walt joins the American Red Cross Ambulance Corps.

1920—Walt and his friend, Ub Iwerks, start their own cartoon business. They create Laugh-O-Grams.

1923—Walt and Roy begin Disney Brothers Studio in California.

1925—Walt marries Lilly Bounds.

1928—Mickey Mouse is created.

1932—Walt receives his first Academy Award Oscar.

1937—*Snow White and the Seven Dwarfs* opens.

1941—The U.S. Army takes over Walt's studio for eight months during World War II.

1955—Disneyland opens in California on July 17.

1966—Walt Disney dies on December 15.

Words to Know

animation (an-i-MAY-shuhn)—cartoons made by quickly presenting drawings, one after another, so that the characters seem to be moving

apprentice (uh-PREN-tiss)—someone who learns a trade or craft by working for a skilled person

classical (KLASS-uh-kuhl)—music such as opera or symphony

employee (em-PLOI-ee)—a person who works for and is paid by someone else

produce (pruh-DOOSS)—to be in charge of putting together a movie or TV program

theme park (THEEM PARK)—a park with rides and attractions based on a certain subject; Disneyland rides are usually based on characters and settings from Disney movies and shows.

trend (TREND)—new fashion or direction in which things are changing

volunteer (vol-uhn-TEER)—to offer to do a job, usually without pay or reward; Walt volunteered for the Red Cross Ambulance Corps.

Read More

Isbouts, Jean-Pierre. *Discovering Walt: The Magical Life of Walt Disney.* New York: Disney Editions, 2001.

Jaffe, Elizabeth Dana. *Walt Disney.* Trailblazers of the Modern World. Milwaukee: World Almanac Library, 2001.

Richardson, Adele. *The Story of Disney.* Built for Success. Mankato, Minn.: Smart Apple Media, 2003.

Useful Addresses

The Walt Disney Company
500 S. Buena Vista Street
Burbank, CA 91521

Walt Disney World
   Guest Relations
PO Box 10000
Lake Buena Vista, FL 32830

Internet Sites

Do you want to find out more about Walt Disney?
Let FactHound, our fact-finding hound dog,
do the research for you!

Here's how:
1. Visit *www.facthound.com*
2. Type in the **BOOK ID** number: **0736822267**
3. Click on **FETCH IT**.
FactHound will fetch Internet sites picked by our editors just for you!

Index